LEO

(From July 23 to August 22)

Horoscope for 2021

Are you a Leo and want to hear more about the astrological forecast for 2021? Consult the 2021 horoscope with the sign Leo. Our astrologer Daniel Sanjurjo reveals to you by decan what 2021 has in store for you.

First quarter horoscope 2021

Resident of V House linked to creation and to the outbursts of the heart, at the start of the year you will be a sad <u>Lion</u> who no longer loves. Sated to nausea, you will no longer find satisfaction in anything. The year 2020 seems to have created in you a painful feeling of emptiness or satiety. The joys that filled you before you will suddenly seem ridiculous. **You can count on the support of your loved ones during these difficult times.** All around you will strive to rekindle the flame that is crackling within you.

Horoscope for the second quarter of 2021

The presence of Neptune in your astral journey shows that a meeting disrupts your daily life when you least expect it. The breath of an air sign will warm your soul and heart. You should not, however, expect everything from this understanding being, but not superhuman. Native of the first decan, you will be clumsy, in all senses of the term ...

Horoscope for the third quarter of 2021

Despite the good waves that will hover around you under the effect of the sparkle of Mars, you will struggle to find your marks. **You will oscillate between cowardice and bravery but will not be able to really define a coherent line of behavior** . Your hierarchy will deem you elusive. Your romantic relationships will match. Sometimes daring, sometimes withdrawn, you will confuse the being who is dear to you. Your behavior may remind him of that of a cat playing with its prey ...

Fourth quarter 2021 horoscope

It is with unexpected hope that you will celebrate the holiday season, **nestled in the comforting shadow of the Moon** . After a year of procrastination, you will regain the upper hand and carry torrents of projects for 2022. Do not regret this year of wandering, you needed a major overhaul to define your priorities. At the end of this existential crisis, you will appear pacified and voluntary!

Love: what the year holds for Leo

Sometimes careless, your head in the air, you will forget important events in the life of your soul mate. The fire of Jupiter will push you to believe that nothing is serious, if not your personal accomplishment ... Single, your desire for glory and domination will keep the contenders away from you. **Far from questioning yourself, you will look with a severe eye and tinged with contempt at those who turn their backs on you** . "They just don't measure up! You are better!" will you declaim, to whoever wants to hear it ...

Leo love horoscope: forecasts for 2021

With his allure of a nonchalant monarch, the Leo has little to worry about when it comes to seduction. Frustrated by a disappointing year, in 2021 he will be keen to make up for lost time. A "banquet" which promises to be wild ...

Work and money: the 2021 forecast for Leo

Encouraged by the planet Pluto, you will develop a keen business sense . You will have "nose" and will make a few winning bets. This clairvoyance will be coupled with a real aptitude for management. You will invest your money wisely to the point of achieving a probable financial tumble! Be careful because this opulence will not go unnoticed. Known to be generous, you could be asked more than necessary by those around you. You must learn to give wisely.

Leo's work horoscope: what's new in 2021?

Ambitious and vaguely domineering, the Lion is not a sign to settle for a second-class place. 2020 having left him with a taste of unfinished business, in 2021 he will put all his energy to use to reinvent himself. An attentive audience will galvanize their desire to always go further.

Leo silver horoscope: what finances in 2021?

If "money is only a fiction" according to Aristotle, the fact remains that it is your favorite story ... and that you would gladly listen to it every night before going to sleep. After a year of crisis, what does 2021 have in store for you?

The health of the sign Leo this year

Under the thumb of House XII, you will experience vertigo, literally and figuratively. **Low blood pressure, inner ear disorders, overwork, you may be subject to loss of balance** . This often reflects an inner unease. It is in your best interest to practice relaxing activities in order to overcome these harmless but somewhat overwhelming weaknesses. Try to log out more often.

The Lion's Family and Friendship Life in 2021

A big hearted lion, you will make sure to **bring your loved ones together** , acting as a catalyst for good humor. Carried by the altruistic outbursts of the Moon, you will ensure the individual development of each member of the family. It is a bit too much. By dint of inquiring about the well-being of others, you sometimes fail to ask yourself if you are happy yourself! In addition, you will sacrifice your partner too regularly for the benefit of your friends or family. It will stir up his resentment.

Leo forecasts for the year 2021 according to your ascendant

Ascendant Leo Aries

You'll be grinning a lot of smiles throughout the first trimester in the hopes of getting the ball rolling. You will be so afraid of falling that you will constantly display a joy of living in the face. You should open up to others instead of keeping your worries to yourself.

Ascendant Taurus

Your Taurus <u>ascendant</u> will be of great help to you in the financial field. He will be your good genius, the one who will dissuade you from squandering your fortune by always hoping for more.

Leo Ascendant Gemini

You won't be taken with a grain of salt, especially as spring approaches. Crushed by the harmful influence of House XII, you will take the fly for everything and nothing - especially for nothing. A little chamomile tea wouldn't hurt you ...

Leo Ascendant Cancer

A mischievous clown will be sleeping inside you all year round, which will be particularly pleasant for those around you! You will always know how to defuse crisis situations by showing a lot of self-deprecation.

Ascendant Leo Virgo

Virgo's common sense will reflect positively on you. Without depriving you of your eccentricities, your Earth ascendant will push you to adapt your behavior to your inter-locutors. This ability to play chameleons will bring you good professional surprises.

Leo Ascendant Libra

In 2021, you will be a perfect illustration of the mirror effect. A real textbook case! You will never cease to blame others for deserting them while you yourself play ghost with your friends.

Ascendant Leo Scorpio

Reliability will not be your strong suit this year! You will make a lot of commitments that you will put off until later and which in the end turn out never to be fulfilled. Promising will be a way for you to get rid of canvassers.

Ascendant Sagittarius

You will be prone to spleen when fall arrives. Under the influence of your parentage, you may be tempted by plans to move or at the very least a vacation. A good idea if we believe the radiation of Jupiter.

Ascendant Leo Capricorn

You will blush a lot if you touch a water sign. Usually lonely, you'll go out of your way to get the attention of a slightly whimsical being. This person will stay with you afterwards, but will not necessarily become your other half.

Leo rising Aquarius

The year 2021 will be for you under the sign of spirituality. Ogre devourer of books, you will increase your knowledge and will be keen to share it. You will seem attracted to new sectors of activity such as education or tourism.

Ascendant Leo Pisces

The year 2021 will be marked by the uneasiness of your soul. Your Pisces ascendant will encourage you to keep a secret that you are burning to reveal.

LEO LOVE COMPATIBILITY

You belong to the astrological sign of Leo and you want to know which signs are compatible with you? Whether we like it or not, we are not all compatible. Some astrological signs are made to love each other, others to hate themselves. Test your romantic compatibility.

LOVE COMPATIBILITY LEO, ARIES

What you like about Aries: His passionate character, his multiple activities, even his hyperactivity, his need to surpass himself and to move forward.

What makes it work: Even if you don't have the same energy, however, you can find yourself on a lot of goals and this can allow you to develop a dynamic relationship full of twists and turns!

What makes that it can not work: Both whole, passionate, inflamed, the tensions, the **rivalries within your couple** are omnipresent and this can lead to you breaking up. A word of advice, learn to put your egos aside! Sex-erotic compatibility: Sign of Fire, passion will be there and the temperature will rise very quickly between you!

LOVE COMPATIBILITY
LEO, TAURUS

What you like about Taurus: His taste for life and good food, his taste for beautiful things or for art, his determination, his sensuality.

What makes that it can work: Beautiful union that here is where the loyalty but also the wise or inflamed passion, the permanent seduction will come to nourish your relation. So you are a beautiful couple.

What makes it can't work: You are both equally possessive, you both want the last word or be right and this easily leads you to conflict, so learn to take responsibility and communicate. The couple is not a competition!

Sex-erotic compatibility: No problem, the elements are all there for each of you to find something for you.

LOVE COMPATIBILITY LEO, GEMINI

What you like about Gemini: His ingenuity, his sense of humor, his presence of mind, his ability to always bounce back.

What makes it work: You know how to motivate each other and projects, outings, hobbies are going well. Thus, you form a very beautiful social couple who know how to share with others their various centers of interest.

So it can't work: One being in action, in control, the other in exchange, recklessness and freedom, you will sometimes have a hard time getting along, but it doesn't is not impossible that you find your balance.

Sex-erotic compatibility: You are in the moment and the Gemini sign is more in the projection, the fantasy. You may not always be in phase. You will therefore have to learn to tune your violins.

LOVE COMPATIBILITY
LEO, CANCER

What you like about Cancer: His sensitivity, his paternal instinct, his sense of values, his need to be reassured.

What makes it work: Generally, you complement each other quite well. So, you bring each other and it can be said that you fill each other's gaps. So you should find a certain balance.

What makes that it cannot work: You are rather solar and in fact, in appearance, Cancer is lunar therefore in the imagination, childhood and you will sometimes find it difficult to understand yourself, the solution communication .

Sex-erotic compatibility: You were made for each other, you just have to learn to keep pace with each other.

LOVE COMPATIBILITY LEO, LEO

What you like about Leo: You have many things in common which in fact make you attract each other without knowing it.

What makes it work: You are dynamic, sociable, open, sometimes social or narcissistic but you can make a perfect couple. So you know how to go in the same direction and you evolve almost the same way as you ask for better!

What makes it not work: You need to master, control each other as much and that might cause some problems. Likewise, be less possessive and your couple will walk alone or almost!

Sex-erotic compatibility: You are on the same wavelength and you are one hundred percent compatible!

LOVE COMPATIBILITY
LEO, VIRGO

What pleases you about Virgo: Her calm, refined, serious, stable side, her need to be reassured and supported, her sense of values.

What makes it work: Virgo knows perfectly well how to bring you to your senses and encourage you to ask yourself, as for you you know how to get her out of her reserves and move forward.

What makes it not work: Your relationship on the other hand is not won in advance because you are very different and you will tend to be bored around him. If you want it to work you will need to put some water in your wine!

Sex-erotic compatibility: You don't have the same desires, the same desires, there is little chance that it will actually work!

LOVE COMPATIBILITY
LEO, LIBRA

What you like about Libra: Its sensuality, its taste for beautiful things, its constant search for balance, its need to be reassured.

What makes it work: This is a sign that you should get along well with and share common tastes. As refined as each other, your story can only be worthy of a fairy tale or a romantic story.

What makes it not work: There really isn't a reason your relationship can't work. However, if you are independent, know how to leave freedom to Libra by not being too possessive.

Sex-erotic compatibility: Between sensuality, seduction, your relationship takes on the appearance of real fireworks.

LOVE COMPATIBILITY LEO, SCORPIO

What pleases you about Scorpio: His mysterious side, his sometimes complex surroundings, his frankness, his straightforwardness, his analytical and understanding mind.

What makes it work: Your relationship will not lack twists and surprises, it is also all that will make the charm of your relationship which will be based exclusively on passion and power struggles.

What makes that it can not work: Your problem lies in the very functioning of your couple which passes most often through ups and downs, therefore in fact, confrontations and tensions. So a long term story seems compromised.

Sex-erotic compatibility: If there is compatibility, it is only held by passion and often this turns out to be destructive, even going as far as dependence.

LOVE COMPATIBILITY
LEO, SAGITTARIUS

What appeals to you about Sagittarius: His liveliness, his reactivity, his taste for travel, his energy and his optimism.

What makes it work: You are made to get along because each brings something to the other. Thus, you motivate each other and you know how to help each other in difficult times. You are therefore on the same wavelength.

What It Can't Work: Your tendency to dominate and control is likely to be a problem in your relationship, and if you want to keep Sagittarius by your side, you'll have to learn to give them space.

Sex-erotic compatibility: No doubt, you have a real connivance and you are in symbiosis.

LOVE COMPATIBILITY
LEO, CAPRICORN

What pleases you about Capricorn: His calm, reassuring, sure of himself, fatherly, strong, unshakeable side, his maturity, his reflection on the world.

What makes it work: Capricorn is someone who knows how to ask you, bring you back to basics while supporting you in your daily life or your projects. He is someone you can count on and that does a lot for you.

Which means that it can't work: You don't really play in the same class, you need to show yourself and please, Capricorn is in the opposite direction, consequently, communication problems are there and your couple will suffer!

Sex-erotic compatibility: You don't have the same demands, the same desires and it won't stick! One asking for more than the other!

LOVE COMPATIBILITY LEO, AQUARIUS

What you like about Aquarius: His sense of humanity, his avant-garde spirit, his ingenuity, his openness.

What makes it work: Opposite sign in the **zodiac**, a lot of things you are made to share. Thus, you can form a very beautiful couple and find a perfect balance together since you are complementary.

What makes it not work: If you're meant to be complementary, that doesn't mean you'll be doing your life together.

Thus, it is not uncommon for your couple to be caught up in a lot of misunderstanding because they do not evolve at all in the same sphere. A tip, communicate!

Sex-Erotic Compatibility: Although you are not on the same page, it can stick perfectly!

LOVE COMPATIBILITY LEO, PISCES

What appeals to you about Pisces: His creative mind, his sometimes disturbing and irrational view of the world, his empathy, his sensitivity.

What makes it work: The romanticism and **sensitivity of the Pisces** attracts you and nourishes you in some way just as you can be an engine for them. Thus, your relationship is not incompatible but is not the simplest!

What makes that it cannot work: Not evolving in the same worlds, your relation is far from being gained and your exchanges risk to be enamelled by tensions, conflicts or misunderstandings!

Sex-erotic compatibility: If your solar energy can make Pisces vibrate and if the sensuality of Pisces can give you ideas, nothing is won in advance!

LEO MAN ASTRO PROFILE

The Leo man knows what he wants and isn't afraid to let it know! Yes, but can we only see him as the king of the jungle? Because, he also has his cracks. If you don't believe us, come and read the astrological profile of the Leo man, and you will better understand his character. Who knows, maybe your birth charts are meant to match.

Who is the Leo man?

The king of animals, surrounded by his court, majestic, imposing, handsome, star smile and mane in the wind.

Distinguished, discreet, calm, he controls his nerves and is sure of his effects. He is generous, good-looking, intelligent and original.

Sensitive, he suffers from not being as good as he hopes. Sentimental, he is often heartbroken by his conquests.

He struggles to keep his rank, divides to rule better. He turns out to be difficult, authoritarian and manipulative.

How to seduce the Leo man

Flatter him, yes, but with subtlety. Approve his choices, recognize his strength, smile at his witticisms, love what he likes.

Avoid contradicting him in public, he is very touchy . Keep your distance to make him court you, something he loves.

What should you expect from a Leo man?

To a vain man, who always wants to be right: to calm him down, don't insist ... To an ambitious person, who sets the bar so high that he ends up not seeing it anymore. But beware, he gets discouraged quickly!

To a jealous person, who sees rivals everywhere. Which, in a way, is quite touching. Because in reality he is a great sentimentalist, who devotes a cult to the one he loves!

Even more secrets about astrological signs with our article on Chinese astrology.

Leo character:

Native of Leo, you are dynamic, toned, determined, fast, passionate and you do nothing without interest and without convictions. So to move forward in your life, you need to have a specific purpose. Always in a hurry, you live at full speed and your loved ones have a hard time following you. Curious, you **thirst for knowledge** (in every sense of the word) and you will constantly seek to enrich yourself.

Brilliant, flirtatious, feline, it's hard not to notice you. Hunter, you have a good instinct for survival and you always land on your feet. Sociable, social, social, you take a great interest in going out and all forms of representations. Depending on the component of your theme, you can show a great extraversion, even exuberance.

· Silver:

It is for you a tool which allows you to realize your ambitions and to materialize your desires. Your taste for beauty encourages you to bet on quality and you do not hesitate to put the price in your purchases. If you are not interested in money, you will do everything to afford your ambitions.

· Activity:

Work does not scare you and you never balk at the task. Passionate, enterprising, you need things to move and you run away from monotony or comfort. Your **need to learn** pushes you to constantly question yourself in order to improve your skills.

Leaving no room for failure, you give yourself all the means to achieve your goals. So, ambitious, tenacious and pugnacious, you do not give up easily.

Independent, even solitary, your relations with your collaborators and your superiors are relatively difficult and you have great difficulty in complying with orders. Straight and a little bossy, you don't fear responsibilities. So you have the makings of a true leader.

· **Orientations:**

Military careers (police, army, gendarmerie, etc.), **jobs with responsibilities** (CEO, project manager, company manager, senior official, etc.), liberal activities (lawyer, doctor, psychologist, advisor, etc.), art (theater, cinema, staging ...), decoration, styling, advertising, luxury trade, the world of business and finance, national education ...

· **Friendship:**

Loyal, frank, direct, you are a sincere friend who can be counted on. However wary, do not become your friend who wants. So, before you surrender and **give your confidence** , you test, you observe, and you never fully disclose yourself. You attach great importance to friendship and if you are betrayed you rarely forgive because you expect great honesty from your friends.

· **Affective:**

Passionate, even inflamed, you do not like redundant stories and you prefer to live complicated relationships but so much more intense. So you run away from mediocrity and frivolous relationships. Full, you know what you want and where you are going.

As a couple, you are constant, caring, creative, original and you always find a solution to boost your relationship. Demanding, you have high expectations of your partner. Affectionate and tender, you give a lot and you have a tendency to suffocate your other half at times. Your relationship is imbued with seduction, sensuality, power struggles and complicity.

· **Well-being:**

You benefit from a good health capital which makes you combative, resistant and tenacious. You know your limits perfectly, which allows you to never push your body too far. Loving to please, you know how to take care of yourself. Your weak points are the back, the spine, the heart, the eyesight, the gall bladder, the pancreas... Your daily anxiety and annoyances often have repercussions on your back, so be careful!

· **Leo Stars:**

Jennifer Lopez , Christophe Willem, Audrey Tautou, Halle Berry, Ben Affleck, Madonna, Mika.

The Leo needs to be admired and to be the center of attention. He likes to show off and have a court gravitate around him like the planets around the Sun.

Domineering, he is proud and determined. He does everything in style and does not usurp his reputation as "have you seen me": he wants people to watch him. Hedonist, he loves life and its pleasures, but likes to share: He is very generous and even broad.

Most of the time, he is kind and courteous and is used to being obeyed: His desires are orders and he can cause great anger if things do not go according to his will.

Volunteer, he knows very early on what he wants in life and will use discipline to obtain it: he spares no effort and has the courage of his ambitions. He can very easily become despotic with those around him, because he waits for everyone to mobilize to help him achieve his dreams: He is well worth it!

He is narcissistically fragile and needs the approving gaze of "his group" to move forward. Tell him he's the tallest and he's going to get there, and he will.

He needs emulation and is dependent on the admiration that one carries him: If one day he receives the acclamations of the crowd, he will not be able to live without.

Loyal, whole and frank, he does not understand slander and pettiness: He is not armed against low blows, but on the other hand, knows very well how to defend himself in the event of a direct attack. It is better not to have him as an adversary. It is cut for excess and grandiose: It is the king of the zodiac!

In love, he is ardent, passionate, generous and idealistic. He is a seducer who often reassures his ego through his conquests. He has a loyal and honest temperament, and likes the social idea of marriage and family: He wants to find a soul mate. However, he is hot-blooded and loves conquest: he will have great difficulty refusing the solicitations of the other sex. A sign of love, he cannot live without it, and if he loses it, he may doubt himself: he needs to be loved.

If the Lion was:

- One color: Golden yellow, orange.
- A metal: Gold
- A stone: Royal topaz.
- An animal: The lion, the eagle, the rooster
- A plant: Sunflower, orange tree.
- A mineral: Diamond
- Part of the body: The heart, back, arterial circulation.
- One country: Italy, Romania, Sicily, Czech Republic, Slovakia, Lebanon, Peru, Cuba, South of France.
- A profession: Jeweler, actor, model, ambassador, croupier, educator, manager of a leisure center.
- One day of the week: Sunday

- A number: 1, 9, 10
- A note: Mi

Leo, your astral love compatibility

- The fire signs (Aries , Leo and Sagittarius) are, in general, quite compatible with Leo , as they are both in greatness and energy. The need for novelty is a driving force that they share, as is the desire to make projects and to be in constant search of intellectual as well as sensual satisfaction.

- With the air signs (Gemini - Libra and Aquarius), Leo can also aim for a beautiful relationship which will be above all based on originality and play. Leo likes to be surprised in Love, and who better than the signs of tune to offer him a relationship that is always on the move and full of twists and turns. The Leo will always respond present as long as we let him breathe!

- The Leo is not content with the good, he wants the best! This little sin of pride undermines his relationship with the earth signs (Taurus , Virgo and Capricorn), because the latter are rather on the reserve and do not appreciate the impetuosity very much. For their relationship to work, the two must bring to the other what is lacking, and thus manage to balance this relationship all in compromise.

- With the water signs (Cancer, Scorpio and Pisces) the Leo risks getting bored, trapped in a straitjacket far too calm for his liking. The water signs are a little too posed for the Leo who is looking for a loving dynamic in constant working order. The relationship can survive if one of the two lets go of their inclinations for the other, but the balance will never be even.

How to seduce a Leo man?

Love is never very simple. The first step is to find the right person. What if the stars get involved? Our astrologer gives you all the keys to understand and seduce a Leo man according to his astral chart.

Who is the Leo man?

He is a flamboyant, solar being who likes to shine, who likes to please.

Because of this, love is very important to him.

If he likes to receive, he also likes to give. Thus, behind his sometimes egocentric side , he is a being with a big heart who can be very generous.

He is not a loner because in a way he needs others to live and flourish.

Where to meet the Leo man?

In the latest fashionable place, in a social place ... You have the chance to meet him at the theater, at the opera, in the new trendy restaurant in the area ...

So, if you want to fall in love with a Leo, go out, move, go to places frequented by beautiful people.

How to seduce the Leo man?

Monsieur is a born hunter. As much to tell you that the flirtation , in all its forms, he knows and he will see you coming for miles.

That said, tell yourself that who does not try anything has nothing. So how do you make him succumb to your charm? By stroking it with the grain, most certainly but not only ...

Know how to titillate his senses, whet his appetite, be sparkling, lively and optimistic ...

He is a man who, even if he seeks to have a certain control over the course of the seduction, also likes the suitors who are sometimes daring.

The first date with the Leo man:

Choose a bright place, lulled by a soft and lively atmosphere. Opt for a trendy and sparkling place that will dazzle your evening.

To love, you need to be fascinated or to feel that you are "wielding" a certain power, even a certain admiration. Feeling loved is your holy grail. Thus, you will aspire to be "pampered" without being "suffocated".

As a good sign of Fire, you are passionate about looking for the intensity of emotions. Seduction is your mode of communication and games of looks are your weapons.

The sign of Leo in love

Sign of Fire, ruled by the Sun, you like to dominate and therefore have a certain ascendant over your partner. So you set the direction of your relationship, which doesn't mean your other half shouldn't take initiatives.

If you enjoy conducting your hugs, you are not saying no to sometimes being directed or referred. You like to "roar" with pleasure and you are a "greedy".

Leo and sex, what is it like?

He's a man who needs to be told he's the best lover "in the world." As much to tell you that he gives himself the means to leave an unforgettable memory of himself. If during the preliminaries , he likes to purr, during the embrace, the latter roars.

He has a **strong libido** and therefore he has great needs. At the same time sensual, seductive and solar, he will try to impress you. Be careful not to idealize him too much because he is a man who, if he knows how to be creative by scratching or biting, can show great classicism.

The fantasies of the sign Leo

Watching each other make love by installing a large mirror in front of his bed. Love in the open air or in a public place.

Erogenous zones in Leo

The chest, abdomen, ears, lower back ...

Your favorite sexual practice according to your astrological sign

Each sign of the horoscope has its own sexual practice! Everything changes depending on whether you are Aquarius, Gemini or Virgo...

The former prefer role-playing games, the others the threesome and the latter sadomasochism. The sex horoscope gives you many ideas to satisfy your fantasies. Nothing better to spice up your married life!

If you've always dreamed of having sex on a boat , that's normal, you are Pisces! Aries are more followers of naturism. Because yes, your astrological sign influences your sex life **!**

Each astrological sign has its own sexual practice

- **Aquarius:** Role play

You don't give a damn about what other people think and you are enjoying life to the fullest. You are never afraid to try new things .

Why not try out the role play then ? With your partner you pretend to be two complete strangers.

In addition to exciting you, this fantasy develops your creativity. How long will you manage to play the game? It's up to you to decide.

. Fish: Making love on a boat

Titanic has left its mark! Nothing very surprising since you are a water sign . Sensitive by nature, you let yourself be rocked by the waves. Little by little, you start to fantasize.

Are you two explorers ready to discover a desert island? Two bird watchers who fell in love on their way to an expedition in the Galapagos? Two first-class passengers ready to go to the captain's dinner? You understand, on a boat, all fantasies are allowed .

. **Aries:** Nudist vacations for adults

Not much shocks you anymore and you are comfortable enough with your body for an adult nudist vacation .

Few people intimidate you, you will easily start a discussion with other couples. In addition, you are very proud of your body and that of your partner. So why not share it with everyone?

. **Cancer:** Painting your body with paint

What could be hotter than experimenting with new things with your partner, while creating art? Let him run through your body with his fingers full of paint. Together, you shape a work and your sensitive side loves it!

. **Virgo:** Being domineering

You always knew deep down that you are a super hot dominatrix . Showing your partner that secret side of you will drive them crazy.

He's just waiting for you to take matters into your own hands. You feel liberated. No more fear of the gaze of others: you were born to be a leader.

· **Libra:** Testing Orgasmic Meditation

You like it when things take their time and are intense. The orgasmic meditation is for you!

This form of yoga allows you to refocus on the deep pleasure of both partners. A 15-minute session to experience a real sexual connection for two .

· **Sagittarius:** Replay sex scenes from your favorite movies

You don't take yourself too seriously, and you're not afraid of ridicule. So spend an entire weekend replaying sex scenes from your favorite movies.

What will it be? The 50 Shades torture chamber , Ghost's pottery blow, or frolics in a wheat field like in Match Point?

Before you start prepare a small list of your favorite scenes. Complicity, giggles, excitement guaranteed!

· **Capricorn:** Eating food on the other's body

For you gourmets! Open the fridge and grab the strawberries, liquid chocolate, whipped cream ...

All you have to do is place these treats on the body parts of your choice. Lick, swallow, suck ... it's up to you!

What astrological sign for a threesome?

· **Gemini:** Having a threesome with your partner

The threesome is made for you dear Gemini! You who are easily bored, you will not be disappointed by the many possibilities offered by this sexual practice. Observe, participate, change partners, the choice is yours.

· **Leo:** Being the patch for a threesome

Many couples are looking for the perfect partner for a threesome . It's you ! Expect to be pampered as it should be. Indeed, without you, this threesome wouldn't even exist.

Have fun and show off what you can do. Now is not the time to back down, when your audience is already at your feet!

· **Taurus:** Watching other couples have sex at a sex party

No one knows, but you are a voyeur. Instead of throwing yourself head first, you prefer to observe.

To learn more, go to a sex party with your partner. Promise yourself to only watch when you arrive.

Resisting will turn you on even more and you will be able to reproduce what you have seen at home. Next time, you will go there and join the party.

· **Scorpio:** Taking the place of your partner

For a long time now you have liked to reverse the roles . You've already gone through your domineering phase, long before the success of 50 Shades of Gray.

You'll love swapping roles with your guy. To do this, take a strapon dildo and test the penetration!

>> All you have to do is take the plunge!

Which sign are you most sexually compatible with?

Believe it or not, sexual compatibility would also depend on your astrological sign! Indeed, sex is not just a matter of physical attraction. It requires being spiritually aligned with your partner. Some signs complement each other better than others. Aries, Taurus or Cancer? Now is the time to find out which astrological sign you have the best sexual chemistry with!

Astrological signs with the best sexual chemistry

- Aries and Libra compatibility **: a couple at the service of the other**

In life, as in love, when an Aries wants something, he doesn't go four ways.

Unlike Libra, who will think, weigh the pros and cons, before making a decision.

She is best placed to channel the fiery character of Aries a bit. The latter, thanks to his determination and unfailing optimism, manages to relax Libra.

Together, they form an **atypical couple** , but a couple that works. Curious about each other, they respect each other a lot.

In bed, they are very attentive to the desires of the other and do everything to **make their fantasies come true** .

- Compatibility Gemini and Sagittarius **: a couple who are not afraid of anything**

Gemini and Sagittarius are the most electric couple ever! It's very simple, together they are not afraid of anything.

Making love outside , using sextoys, having a threesome... no problem! The more daring and daring the fantasy, the more they will want to realize it.

These two signs are delighted to have found in the other a gaming partner ready to try all the follies.

- Taurus and Scorpio compatibility **: a couple of epicureans**

When making love, Taurus and Scorpio have all their senses on the alert. Together, they form one of the most sensual duets.

The attraction of Scorpios for intimacy mingles perfectly with the **carnal desires** of Taurus. These two have a hard time leaving the room when they do.

Their lovemaking is so sensual it looks like it came straight out of a movie.

Which astrological sign to have sex with?

- Cancer **and Capricorn** compatibility : **when opposites attract**

No one embodies this adage better than these two signs. Cancerians are imaginative, teasing, dreamy ... unlike serious, determined and down to earth Capricorns.

Both are on the opposite end of the **astrological sign** spectrum . Yet their connection is very strong. They find the other's personality exotic and fascinating.

Their **romantic relationship** is quite tumultuous and passionate as they have to share their fantasies with someone very different. But everything always ends up working out.

- Leo and Aquarius compatibility : **a couple that has spice**

Leo people are quite selfish and they don't like people trying to control them. They do everything to have someone in their bed to **satisfy their desires** .

This of course gives rise to complicated situations, in particular for their partners: one-sided relationship, **love disappointment** , broken heart ...

Aquarians are the only ones who can put them back in their place. They shine by their intelligence and by their detachment.

They intrigue the Leo, who gradually feel that they are no longer in control. And they're starting to like it.

In bed, Aquarians always have unexpected ideas, which Leo are quick to satisfy.

- Compatibility Virgo and Pisces : **the most unexpected couple**

Virgos are distant, pragmatic, logical and down to earth. Pisces, on the other hand, live in a fairy tale and are a little upside down.

Yet they complement each other wonderfully. They tone down the excessive personality traits of the other and share the same sense of humor.

An adjective to describe their antics? Savages. Together, they are finally able to let their guard down and let go completely.

Pisces are ready to test anything and they are delighted to have found in the other the **perfect partner** to do so.

They'll never tell you what's going on behind their bedroom door, but trust us, things are happening!

Your ideal sexual position according to your astrological sign

Are you more of the doggy style, missionary, Amazon, Andromache? You may not know it, but your astrological sign greatly influences your choices when it comes to sex positions. Yes Yes ! Whether you are Pisces, Cancer, or Libra, not all of you reach orgasm the same way. So what will it be for you?

The astrological signs who prefer the classic Kamasutra positions

- **Aries: the position of the Andromache**

The **Aries woman** is a go-getter and she loves to take the lead. N-either one nor two, she climbs on her partner and imposes her rhythm.

He is at the height of excitement in front of this confident and passionate woman. In addition, the panoramic view of her breasts and the possibility of grabbing her buttocks, are not to displease him. Long live the **position of the Andromache** !

.   **Taurus: the 69**

The **Taurus woman** enjoys giving as much as receiving. Nothing turns her on more than **long foreplay** before moving on to the main course.

Queen of fellatio, she expects a memorable cunnilingus from her partner. To do this, she does not hesitate to express her wishes to him. And he loves it!

.   **Gemini: doggy style**

The Gemini woman is sensual and curious. She's never against a little role play, especially if it involves doggy style.

This position turns her on more than anything because she is self-confident and proud of her body. She loves to imagine the languid gaze of her partner on her pretty buttocks.

.   **Cancer: victory**

The **cancer woman** likes to be as close as possible to her partner. He sits with his legs apart. She, lying on her back, faces him and surrounds his chest with her legs.

He lifts her slightly, grabbing her above the hips. He serves her hard while penetrating her. One of **the most romantic sex positions** !

.   **Fish: the spoon**

The **Pisces woman** is without artifice. She loves the simple things in life and the same goes with Kamasutra.

Acrobatics, very little for her. What she likes ? A position where both partners take as much pleasure as each other.

With the spoon, she is delighted, coiled in the arms of her dear and tender.

· Virgo: the missionary revisited

The **Virgo woman** is quite shy and she needs stability. The missionary is therefore ideal for her!

No need for extravagant positions to get it right! But she's not against spicing things up a bit.

She sits on the edge of the bed, legs raised, while her partner enters her, legs stretched on the floor. A small variant of the missionary for optimal stimulation of the clitoris.

Astrological signs that love original sex positions

· Leo: the proud queen

The **lion woman** goes full speed and knows what she wants. His favorite position? The proud queen of course!

Sitting astride her partner, she turns her back to him. She sets the tempo and adjusts his movements to hers by grabbing her hips.

The sight of her arch and her buttocks make her lose her mind completely and she knows it well!

· Libra: the Amazon

Romantic and caring, the **Libra woman** loves to make love while looking her partner in the eyes.

He is sitting or lying down, she sits on him sideways, her legs perpendicular to his. This angle of penetration is not without risk, but the sensations are worth it!

His hands are free and come to walk along the curve of his beautiful ... And that, she loves!

· Scorpio: all positions

The **Scorpio woman is** not afraid of anything, just one thing, boredom! Her partner must be ready to surprise her, otherwise she takes the reins not to let go.

Doggy style, Amazon, union of the butterfly, semi-wheelbarrow ... Everything is good to reach orgasm !

· Sagittarius: scissors

The **Sagittarius woman** is always very independent, even in a relationship. But that doesn't mean she's selfish in bed, she just likes to be taken care of.

She lies on her back at the edge of a table, legs stretched out, crossed and raised. Her standing partner grabs her ankles and spreads her legs slightly.

While he penetrates her, she can stimulate her clitoris . Double pleasure!

· Capricorn: the rocking horse

Quiet, reserved and suspicious, the **Capricorn woman** finds it difficult to give herself up. She therefore needs to feel confident to reveal herself.

What does she prefer? Positions where she is closest to her partner, such as the rocking horse.

He is sitting cross-legged, his hands behind his back. She sits astride him, squeezing him firmly with her thighs.

As she goes at her own pace, she feels good. She takes the opportunity to stroke the hair of her partner, while he admires her breasts.

· Aquarius: the sedan chair

The **Aquarius woman** is an artist. She's not afraid to experiment with acrobatic sexual positions to achieve nirvana.

Like the sedan **chair** . She leans outstretched arms on the bed. The man, standing behind her, lifts her by the hips, then wedges his legs under his arms.

A kind of raised doggy style! Nothing to worry about the Aquarius woman ...

This is the astrological sign most likely to lie and cheat

We are far from the idea of stigmatizing certain signs of the zodiac, but we still have to reveal the difficult truth to you. An astrological sign would be more likely than the others to cheat on its other half, and to lie.

Each human being is unique, of course. But we do share character traits , flaws, qualities, and for many people it depends on our **date of birth** .

The most unfaithful sign

From there to saying that there are points in common between the natives of the signs, there is only one step, which we cross easily. According to a recent survey, when it comes to **loyalty** and honesty in love, not all zodiac signs are created equal.

If you're hesitant to ask for their zodiac sign on your date on the first date, this is going to make you want to do it. The **extra-marital dating** site **IllicitEncounters.com** carried out a study among its 180,000 subscribers, to group them by astrological sign.

16% of those registered on the site (therefore a priori unfaithful to their partner or companion) are native to the sign of Capricorn .

The classification of unfaithful astrological signs

Just behind Capricorns, another sign stands out. 13% of those registered on the extra-marital dating site IllicitEncounters.com are **Libra** . On the third step of the podium of the least faithful signs, we find the Cancer.

Conversely, the trio of the most faithful signs are Sagittarius , Aquarius and **Pisces** .

The site also provided a ranking of the signs most likely to be deceived. This is the sign of **Leo** . There you have it, now you know why many people choose their partner based on their astrological sign.

What if your soul mate is your opposite sun sign in astrology?

You do not know, but in anti-Zodiac signs astrology draws... And as they learn to discover each other a long and intense romantic relationship begins.

Astrology is a perfect place to learn to understand. The same goes for loved ones! The stars help us to better identify our relationship to them, but also the tensions we have trouble understanding. What if astrology helped you find love?

What are the anti-Zodiac signs?

We grant you: it's not always easy to access the astral, ascending, and other charts of the one you loved at night. However, having the astrological sign is better! This first measure will let you know your crush's deep essence, or personality. And recognizing his sun sign, you'll know his opposite sign, thanks to our list below.

Many of the Zodiac's signs are opposite to theirs: in general, it has all the opposite features. As two Zodiac signs intersect, an attraction/repulsion interaction also exists. Yet most often the two signals wind up establishing a long and lovely friendship. The contrary signs of astrology:

Aries / Libra

Taurus / Scorpio

Gemini / Sagittarius

Capricorn / Cancer

Aquarius / Leo

Pisces / Virgo

The love-compatibility of Zodiac signs

Take Gemini: he's very indecisive, has a rough time understanding who he's actually deep inside, and he's very adaptable, enjoys conversation and trade, and... He just enjoys the boundaries of legality.

 Instead, we find Sagittarius. The latter knows precisely who he is and knows his principles, justice matters to him: he appears to be moralistic and the debate with him is complex, diplomacy is not his skill...

Therefore the two signals have many variations, but in the area of excitement, the desire to have fun and feel free! A Gemini will develop self-confidence in touch with a Sagittarius, and a Gemini will learn to be more versatile. Result: beyond the early days and exploring their discrepancies, these two signals will put together a lot and go a long way.

Keep your eyes open to see the signs opposite the Zodiac sign!

Astrological signs with the best sexual chemistry

- **Aries and Libra compatibility : a couple at the service of the other**

In life, as in love, when an Aries wants something, he doesn't go four ways.

Unlike Libra, who will think, weigh the pros and cons, before making a decision.

She is best placed to channel the fiery character of Aries a bit. The latter, thanks to his determination and unfailing optimism, manages to relax Libra.

Together, they form an **atypical couple** , but a couple that works. Curious about each other, they respect each other a lot.

In bed, they are very attentive to the desires of the other and do everything to **make their fantasies come true** .

- **Compatibility Gemini and Sagittarius : a couple who are not afraid of anything**

Gemini and Sagittarius are the most electric couple ever! It's very simple, together they are not afraid of anything.

Making love outside , using sextoys, having a threesome... no problem! The more daring and daring the fantasy, the more they will want to realize it.

These two signs are delighted to have found in the other a playing partner ready to try all the follies.

- **Taurus and Scorpio compatibility : a couple of epicureans**

When making love, Taurus and Scorpio have all their senses on the alert. Together, they form one of the most sensual duets.

The attraction of Scorpios for intimacy mingles perfectly with the **carnal desires** of Taurus. These two have a hard time leaving the room when they do.

Their lovemaking is so sensual it looks like it came straight out of a movie.

Which astrological sign to have sex with?

- **Cancer and Capricorn compatibility : when opposites attract**

No one embodies this adage better than these two signs. Cancerians are imaginative, teasing, dreamy ... unlike serious, determined and down to earth Capricorns.

Both are on the opposite end of the **astrological sign** spectrum . Yet their connection is very strong. They find the other's personality exotic and fascinating.

Their **romantic relationship** is quite tumultuous and passionate as they have to share their fantasies with someone very different. But everything always ends up working out.

· **Leo and Aquarius compatibility : a couple that has spice**

Leo people are quite selfish and they don't like people trying to control them. They do everything to have someone in their bed to **satisfy their desires** .

This of course gives rise to complicated situations, in particular for their partners: one-sided relationship, **love disappointment** , broken heart ...

Aquarians are the only ones who can put them back in their place. They shine by their intelligence and by their detachment.

They intrigue the Leo, who gradually feel that they are no longer in control. And they're starting to like it.

In bed, Aquarians always have unexpected ideas, which Leo are quick to satisfy.

BY DANIEL SANJURJO

www.ingramcontent.com/pod-product-compliance
Lightning Source LLC
Chambersburg PA
CBHW061321140726
47998CB00006B/2491